A Rogue's Guide to Acquisition:
Principles from the Final Frontier

By Jayesh Mehta and Ranak Jones

Forward written by Anish Sikri

Cover Design by Omplyfydfx
www.omplyfydfx.com

www.BalancedUniverse.com

Printed in the United States of America
First Printing, 2012

ISBN 978-0-9856529-0-6

www.BalancedUniverse.com

This book is dedicated to Perry Farrell, who reawakened my passion for writing long ago.

-Jayesh Mehta

Table of Contents

Forward

"Red Alert! Shields up! Transfer all power to phasers, and arm the photon torpedoes…" Sound familiar? These phrases sound like words coming from Captain Jean-Luc Picard of the USS Enterprise. A captain could use these words during an emergency – it is during this moment that the captain has to make a split-millisecond decision among various choices/options presented to him/her. Any one choice is the difference between success and failure. Failure is not an option. Keep in mind; I have said failure, not retreat. Understanding the difference between failure and retreat is paramount. A retreat is a calculated move to minimize risk – which allows one to regroup and face the challenge at hand again, whereas failure is not understanding risk at all.

After review of all the available solutions (no matter how absurd they may seem) Captain Picard makes a final decision (to the best of his knowledge and abilities). He makes it and no one in his crew questions his leadership. Just because he is the captain doesn't make his decision absolute. He had to work very hard to earn that leadership role from his crew. Throughout his career in Starfleet, one can see that he knows how to manage responsibility and authority. Those two elements go hand in hand.

The word "leadership" is used loosely in every nook and corner of the world. Laggard leadership/performance results in a dilution of the word. There is a good ole saying in Spiderman (quite cliché by today's standard, but still a timeless phrase), that is "with Great Power, Comes Great Responsibility". This is what solid leadership is all about.

Today, where do you see effective leaders as the pillars of industry? My bet is it would be seen in a small number of companies as compared to the whole market group.

This is one of the main books to read in order to become a very effective businessperson. One's library should definitely contain books by Robin Sharma, Dale Carnegie, Napoleon Hill, William J. O'Neil, Warren Buffet, Richard Branson, Sun Tzu, Walter Isaacson's Steve Jobs, and Rudolph W.

Giuliani – these guys are master at executing their goals and vision.

"A Rogue's Guide to Acquisition" is the first book in a series, which provides some edgy way of looking at things – and encouraging the reader to execute their plans to go to the top. In life, not everything is black and white, when it comes to playing the game…you could be correct in everything, and still lose – that is life…shit happens. This book illuminates the different shades of the grey path between the black and white ways of thinking.

You have to have the walk, the talk, and be able to back it up to be successful. Not everyone can walk the walk, talk the talk, and back it all up. The majority may do one or two of the elements, but that is not how you are going to win the corporate game. You need all three elements.

Run like Bolt. Dance like MJ. Fight like Ali. Lead without a title like Robin Sharma. Play like Jordan. Trade like William O'Neil. Have a vision like Steve Jobs. Dominate like Branson. Strategize like Jayesh and Ranak.

This book is for all the underdogs, the dreamers, entrepreneurs, the visionaries, upcoming hedge fund/VC/PE managers, students, who have not made it big yet, but will get there soon. This guide will aid in kicking your ass, so that you get off that couch/plateau that you are stuck on – so you can reach your full potential to dominate whatever industry you want to be in.

STUDY this book! After that study a few other books (hint is in this forward)....and Rule like a Rogue!

Anish Sikri

Introduction

We know most people will probably skip over this and get to the meat of the book, but for those of you reading this we will explain some of the thought processes, assumptions, etc. that went into the book. First and foremost, this is not strictly a book of what is, rather it is an interpretation of what is. In this, we mean that you may read some of the principles and come up with a totally different interpretation than we did. Or you may read those interpretations and think we may only be touching on what the full meaning is. This doesn't mean we don't know what we're talking about. We are basing everything on our experiences, our knowledge, the news, etc. This also does not mean you are wrong…misguided maybe, but not wrong. We kid. Everything is fluid and up for debate, so if you do, let's discuss via http://www.balanceduniverse.com.

Secondly, Ranak is the ass. He doesn't deny it, embraces it even. Ranak will be sarcastic. He will make comments that some may find mean. This is all done in mostly fun. You will see us making fun of engineers…a lot. Why? Do we hate them? No, they are the ones who advance their species. We could make fun of the salespeople, but then we'd probably be pissing off our main readers. We could make fun of the accountants, but they have no sense of humor. We can't make fun of the administration staff…they're the gatekeepers…never mess with a gatekeeper. And we can't make fun of the executives, they could really frell us with litigation, black balling, and so on. Engineers probably are not reading this, unless they mistook this as some sci-fi book. Engineers typically are used to getting made fun of, and sometimes use self-deprecating humor. Plus, what's an engineer going to do, not fix a coupler?

Thirdly, you'll notice that the numbering doesn't start at 1. Don't worry, you did get the whole book. There are another twenty principles that were lost, and have been recently uncovered, and will be released at a later time. So why release these twenty-one principles now instead of waiting for the others? We're impatient. Also, twenty-one has the first two prime numbers in it, and the two most powerful numbers multiplied equal it: 3 and 7. Plus as Gint had done, it is a good marketing ploy.

Fourthly, we have borrowed information from different universes. We would like to thank them for giving us material we could infuse into the text. There are references from many Sci-Fi TV, movie, and books as well as some from conspiracy theorists. If you are a representative of one of those, please do not sue us. If we were to note down every reference, there would be so many footnotes to put in, our heads probably would explode. We will name some of them here, and if we forget any, we apologize: Star Trek, Star Wars, Babylon 5, Flash Gordon, Dr. Who, Stargate, V, Firefly/Serenity, Farscape, Andromeda, Battlestar Gallactica, Enemy Mine, Alien Nation, Space 1999, Earth: Final Conflict, Hitchhiker's Guide to the Galaxy, Space: Above and Beyond, Isaac Asimov, Philip K. Dick, Robert Charles Wilson, Frank Herbert/Dune, and Joe Halderman.

Fifthly, this book is written in a conversational tone. There will be times that proper grammar takes a back seat in the interest of flow. There will also be times that something seems misspelled or the wrong homophone, but trust me, everything is spelled the way we meant it to be spelled. For example, the foreword is spelled forward as an homage, to what, you will have to find out for yourselves. This book will make you look terms up. We intended this to be interactive, so utilize the Web.

Sixthly, ethics be ghuy. Ethics are subjective to the time, culture, planet, and person. Ethics are very rarely used in business. The only time they are used is if it is known that it may harm them. If a merchant can get away with it, they will. Sometimes they get caught, most times they do not. Most business books will either tell you to be ethical, or they will skirt the issue. We don't advise breaking laws and such, but there is a lot of gray area between the truth and the law, and if you want to be successful, you have to navigate in that gray. Pick and choose what is best for you. This is about reality, not some holo-deck fantasy world where everybody plays by the rules. Profit is profit.

Principle 21

**Once you have their money
... never give it back.**

You may be thinking, "well, yeah, but how do we do that? We have guarantees and warranties, blah, blah, blah." This doesn't mean you don't hand them their money back, just make sure you have a string attached to it, to snatch it back (and, no, not literally... usually). Make it as uncomfortable or inconvenient as you can for the customer. They may have legitimate reasons to want their money back, and if they do, they will go through the trouble of being inconvenienced. If it's not hard, then everyone will do it. Profit is what you want, and you can't have it if everyone gets there money back.

Let's say you have a customer who wants their money back. What are you going to do, you've already spent it? O' woe is you. Did you give them a guarantee? Is there any way out of it, without violating any laws (put the phaser away!)? Can you blame someone else, like the Faruun who made it? (Let those insignificant peon ship-builders pay for it!) If you're really nice, and do give them their money back, will they buy something else from you, or will they say 'frell you' and walk away? These are the questions you need to ask yourself.

First, there are only a couple of reasons to offer a guarantee: one, for lower priced items with the thought process that the customer won't bother returning it because it's not worth their time because the cost is so low (how many star cruisers have a money-back guarantee?), or because the product is perfect (and if you believe that, you are either naive, delusional, or both). You say, "Well I can return my 1000 bucks holoscreen to my local Nlvqu' Je'!" Well, yeah, they have many different products, and many that are competitors of each other; they know the customer will probably buy another, different brand from them. Most of us don't offer our competitor's items.

You could just replace the item, thereby never giving back their hard cash, or you could offer them a discount or credit for next time. Replacing the item will cost you that item and still may piss off the customer. This makes them a drain and loses them as repeat business. If you give them a discount or credit the next time, then you lose no money on the first sale, and only lose a small amount on the next sale…but you might piss them off, and they won't come back at all, still keeping their money on the first sale, but losing them as customers and having them call you a zarking hazmot, possibly losing other customers' revenue.

Wow, you must be saying, you've just bashed each technique to deal with disgruntled customers, so how do you keep the money of all your sales? Well you can do an "as-is" policy, maybe where the contract specifically states that satisfaction is not guaranteed, but you'll probably lose repeat sales. There is no perfect way or policy. The universe is fluid, and you have to change with the flow, or be swept away by the tides. It all depends on your business, what you are willing to trade off, etc. In the Service industry, you really can't exchange an item, or just give them a refund (unless they're real pains in the ass, and not worth your time). What you could offer is credit on the next time they contract your services or just go with the "as-is" policy.

Turning upset customers into happy, repeat customers is always good, but your time is worth money, and the more time you deal with upset customers, the less time you spend with new customers, so whatever your policy, do it quickly. We are all beggars, we just ask for different things. Businesses ask for sales, the customers ask for deals, or in remorse their money back. Does the beggar give back his coins? I dare you to ask a beggar on the street for your quarter back.

Principle 22

Never pay more for an acquisition than you have to.

You may be thinking, no shit. Who wants to pay more than they have to? Well, yeah, but it's still a rule, and is one of the hardest to stick to. Sometimes you're going to be in a rush, and have to pay more, or more than likely, just don't do enough research. The first thing you have to do is figure out how much you can afford on the acquisition, and how much of your profit it is going to eat. You can figure this out, even if you're not an accountant, for a small, uncomplicated venture…if you have a more complicated, Fizzbin-like, large business, you have accounting departments for this and probably have an underling reading this.

Research…is probably the most important and the least exciting (yes, even more boring than the accounting…at least you can fudge the numbers there). You have to find all the possible sellers of similar acquisitions, compare their prices. Then you have to take the top few and compare their quality. Then you have to differentiate the different features (if there are any). And then you have to check references. Boring, but essential.

As an example, let's take a company, named Pla-kur Yel. This company wants to purchase some automatic locks for its Research and Development Division. They get these high-tech ones at a discount from a salesalien. They install them. Then a month later, they have one of their test subjects escape! How did this happen? They were supposed to be high-tech? Ah, but they bought it from a salesalien that worked for some untrustworthy Browncoat. If they had taken the time to research this, they would not have to pay bounty hunters or use up other valuable resources to get the subject back. It may have been a decent price, but they now have to pay four to five times more and countless delays in research all because they didn't do their due diligence. They thought that no one would scam them. This is a big boy universe, never think you won't be fleeced.

If you're in sales, and think, "Hey, I'm not a buyer, so I don't need this," you may be right…or maybe, just maybe, you can get into the heads of your marks…I mean customers, and find out how much they can afford, what they're looking for, and sell to their needs, rather than selling to your wants. If you know one of your potential clients needs your product right away, you know they have time constraints, and will purchase without doing their due diligence as long as your price is palatable. Or you may have a customer who's a cheap go-se, and loves to get a deal. You can up your price by 10-15%, and let them "talk" you down that percentage. You don't lose, their ego wins. If you do all this thoroughly, then you will rarely pay more than you have to. Or sell for less than you want to.

Principle 23

Beware of the greed for knowledge.

Knowledge is god. Am I a blasphemer? Probably…but in this statement, not so much. This principle is not so much your greed, but for those green blooded hobgoblins that would take your power away. They will cajole you. They will try to use logic. They will try to force it from you. Some think that information should not be that important, so why not share it freely? Their thought is that if everyone knows, then it has no power. We would all be equal. Great a hive mind…no one's gonna rebel against that! Pu-leeze! All it takes is one bit of information more than the next person. And just because you have information, does not mean you have knowledge. We are not Utopia, greed is real, and you need to protect yourself.

People will try to disable your knowledge because knowledge can give you all the power to succeed, although it's not guaranteed (see perfect products in #21). The difference is that with a lack of knowledge, you will fail, and that's what they want. The good thing for you is that most people don't know how to use the information they get, and turn it to their advantage. You may have an engineer that can create a jetpack out of some gum and Bio-mimetic gel, but without the knowledge of how to procure the gel at a good price, market the product, etc., he might as well chew the gum and leave the genetic manipulation to the pros. (What? Look it up.)

We are not super-humans with positronic brains, so how can anyone succeed without the capacity of storing every bit of information? Some information is more important than others. You don't need to be an accountant, marketer, salesperson, engineer, technician, computer guru, master coder. You just need to know how to find all of them, let them know you know enough of their jobs to know they're bullshitting. It also doesn't hurt if you have something on them, for a rainy day. If you happen to be one of these professionals…well then, I'm sorry. No, seriously, if you are one of these professionals, you need to know as much about that profession as possible. Any new theories, advancements, information; you need to either have introduced it, or you need to be the one introducing it to your company at the right time.

Timing is another component of knowledge. You may know that some cybernetic corporation is putting out some new technology for the public. You could jump on it right away, and incorporate it into your company…and if it fails, your ass is gone. You don't want to be the guinea pig, it may have been better to wait to make sure all the bugs are out, and you're not all assimilated…but then again, if you wait too long, you may be viewed as too cautious and conservative, and eventually a relic.

So essentially, you need the right information, a way to utilize the information and some good timing. In addition, luck doesn't hurt every so often. You also need to keep that information to yourself until you can use it to your advantage. Wait, you say, I've got a boss who is a complete idiot, how is he above me and/or others who have way more knowledge then him… Well, sometimes nepotism, kissing ass, and a little back-stabbing will get idiots into high positions, but they will eventually either fail, or stagnate, or be smart enough to have some knowledgeable people underneath them who have no timing or drive to move beyond where they are...complacency is easy...it's like marrying the first person that asks you, it's just easy, until you realize that you're 50 and never lived life.

Complacency is like getting drunk, you kill a bunch of brain cells, you think you're happy, at least for a while, and all is good until you wake up next to Butter Face. Enough with the metaphors for now, if you're reading this, then you're either not complacent, trying to get out of complacency, a sci-fi geek looking for references to your favorite show/movie, or some random schmuk who's extremely bored and found the title interesting (sorry). Remember: There is no ignorance, there is knowledge.

Principle 24

Trust is the biggest liability of all.

People will screw you. Businesses will screw you. The governments will screw you. Your family will screw you. Your spouse will screw you…and maybe some others as well…my advice, talk to your counselor about that. Basically everyone and anyone will screw you if you trust them too much. You may think that you have to trust someone; otherwise, you'd be a paranoid ass. Well hee-haw. This is business.

If you were a multi-billionaire, would you get married to someone without a prenup? Especially if said someone has about two billion less than you do? Yeah, you don't have that much, but if you're planning to make money, then you may want to think about getting one. In business, it's the same. This is not to say that you tell no one anything, but that whomever and whatever you tell will not come to bite you in the ass tomorrow. Always have a contingency plan. And have a contingency for that plan as well. This is about being prepared, and in the end, it is all about CYA. The best way to do this is to not trust anyone 100%.

Trust ties into knowledge. If you give away your knowledge, you give away your power/advantage. You dilute the power of the knowledge. The knowledge is no longer as useful. You then have a useless waste of memory space in your head. Keep little bits of information to yourself. You may have a business partner or colleague that is a friend of yours. Great! Talk to them, joke with them, but never give everything to them. Would you give them all your money and trust them to pay your bills, buy your food, and save a little for your retirement. If you do, then can I be your friend…fekkik! Let's say you have some information that could help your business, and you tell your colleague about it. What's stopping them from claiming that information as their own? So never trust anyone completely. And watch out for the corps who will lull you into trust, and the shadows who would abuse it.

Principle 25

There's nothing more dangerous than an honest businessperson.

Do I want you to lie? Maybe, although that would be unethical of me to do. What I'm telling you is to not tell the truth all the time. To omit information that may harm you, or imply information that may help you. Let's take a salesperson perspective. Let's say you are selling warp drives. Your competitors may have had a very high profile failure of a couple of drives because of a coupling. You may tell your customers that ours haven't failed because of couplings. While this is true, your engines may have failed due to coolant issues, but you don't mention that. This gives the impression that your engines don't fail, and puts into your customer's mind that your competitor's do. You have not lied. You have just selectively given or withheld information (see knowledge is god). This is a very blatant and somewhat overblown example, and some may consider unethical…but show me a completely ethical salesperson, and I'll show you a failure (kidding…kind of).

Everybody withholds truth, and many lie, although not all the time, and not in every situation. The wife may ask the husband if a particular item of clothing makes them look fat. The husband may reply A) with a lie, "No, honey, you look great" or some variation; B) with the truth, "Yes" and may involve some pain; or 3) with an omission of truth, "That dress is slimming" or some variation. Which answer is better? More ethical? Will get you into the least amount of trouble? You need to make the decision of what is best for you...but my advice is always use selective information, gives me a clear conscience and involves less pain.

Well, how is the honest businessperson dangerous? The honest businessperson will always tell the truth, even if they don't have to. You may think, that, hey, I'd like to work for him, always get the truth...are you sure you want that, especially if they are unpleased with your work, or more importantly, when your product has a flaw (see perfect product). He will tell the customer this, and more than likely lose the customer (although the customer may appreciate the honesty, who wants to buy a warp drive that they know has a flaw). Beyond this, there is also the point that most businesspeople are not honest or ethical. They will take the honest businessperson's customers if and when they can. Eventually the honest businessperson will either fail, or never advance past where they are now.

What about the honest businessperson as a customer? Well that's not so bad, although they may be stricter on your honesty, or perceived honesty (so if you know the warp drive doesn't work past 5, then you'd either better tell them, or not want them as a repeat customer). We don't live in a Utopian galaxy, therefore you have to assume that the other side is not being completely truthful, and you must keep your guard up and only release what you need to. "Any fool can be honest; it is only what he knows. The wise are aware of when to share the truth."

Principle 26

The quiet ones are the ones that change the universe... The loud ones only take the credit.

You know the type…the loudmouth who talks about how he knew of the collective when the collective was still just a nanomachine. Or the guy that asks for your ideas, shoots them down, then a month later presents it to the higher ups as his own idea…while telling them you are no better than a squatting Drac. Or the person who promises you the stars and hands you a bag of shit. This isn't a rule that says shut your mouth. It means don't get diarrhea of the mouth. Be shrewd. Be cunning. Use your knowledge and timing. Talk when you need to, not just because you can.

It's also about impressions. No one likes to be dominated in a conversation, least of all your clients. You are trying to sell to them, not get a job with them, so shut your mouth for a while, and listen to them. Make them feel like the center of the universe. If you're the buyer, you still need to listen rather than talk, make your suppliers feel overconfident, you may be able to coax out a better deal.

We all like to get credit for things we have done. Getting that little pat on the back, a congratulatory high-five, an increase in rank, etc. Do you need to get that from everyone? If so, I suggest talking to your counselor about your need for acceptance, and low self-worth. For the rest of us, we want the acknowledgment for something done well. If you're a salesperson, do you need acknowledgment from Engineering? Only if they have the boss's ear (and no not literally, that's just gross!). We need the acknowledgment from the people we care about (yes, you can consider your spouse or other significant other). Mainly you want the people who can help you advance yourself to give you credit. You know who they are, so I won't go listing them. One caveat to taking credit, it can easily to turn to blame, so beware what you claim.

The most important thing about being quiet and not loud is that you can draw less attention to yourself when you need to. The less attention they have on you, the more they will say in front of you. The more they say, the more information and knowledge you get. When the timing is right, you can unleash the information, get your credit, but more importantly, advance yourself.

You could be advancing within the company, or advancing your company through information, profits, etc. You must be thinking, "What, I'm supposed to be quiet, how the hell will anyone notice me!" If you yelled that, give yourself one demerit for not listening. The point is to not be so loud and self-important (there will be more on that later), talk, socialize, take credit when it's due, do all the things you normally do, but listen. Be aware of your surroundings, and use that to your advantage. How many people do you see that are "loud" that succeed in the long run. Oh sure, they'll throw some jargon around, but eventually people will realize how much bullshit is being heaped on them, and they will fail (probably go to another company and do the same thing over again, eventually exhausting their opportunities). We all know that a certain amount of BS works, but the loud will bury themselves in it, whereas the successful will put it in front of the bay doors, light it, and after the engineer stomps it out, call it a cake. And have them believe it. And thank you for it. (The real test is if you can do this with the higher ups... engineers crave socialization too much, and will tend to believe anything just so they can talk to someone cooler than them…just kidding! (Unless you're not an engineer, than it's all true).

Principle 27

**Never begin a negotiation on
an empty stomach.**

You may be laughing about this, but it's true. Think about it, you go into a negotiation/meeting and things are progressing. All of the sudden there's a loud rumbling sound...with a little squeak at the end. Everybody looks around to see where the sound came from. Then you hear another rumbling, but from another part of the table...oh hell, now everybody's rumbling. There's a suggestion to break for a meal, and your negotiations that were progressing have been stalled. Now don't you wish you had eaten that candy bar?

Another scenario is that the rumbling happens, and people laugh, tensions are eased, and negotiations progress more rapidly...but at your expense. You will be the butt of their jokes. You will have lost some credibility. You could play it off, but that's extra work that you could be using on other things. If you had eaten a little, you'd have that time, or be making fun of that someone else who went there on an empty stomach.

Looking internally, if you're hungry going into a negotiation, you will make bad choices. You will be hungry, and eager to get out, eat some breen, and drink hot jala. You will be in a rush, miss things, and be more amenable to a bad trade, just so you can get out. This is not good negotiating. If you look through history and different cultures, you will see that most had the tradition of eating before you conduct business. So many could not be wrong.

Although this rule seems to be about hunger, it's actually deeper than that. It is a metaphor for distractions. If you don't eat enough, you're hungry. If you eat too much, you're stuffed and want to curl up in a corner and sleep. If you bring in personal problems, you'll be thinking of those instead of listening. If your customer/fellow negotiator is wearing something provocative/attractive, your mind won't be thinking about anything logical. The list can go on eternally (well, if not that, then a really, really, long time). The point is, check your distractions at the door, so you can do business at the table.

The flip side to this is to distract your counterpart across the table. You can do this with bad BO or breath (you may only get to negotiate once with them if you do this). You can turn up or down the thermostat, and then dress accordingly (only works if it's at your place, and even then, may not distract enough). Or you could put a pair of mivonks down on the table (where and how you got them, I don't want to know). I propose a suggestive dress. You're not a female? Even better! (just see if they can take their eyes off you!)

Principle 28

A wealthy man can afford anything except a conscience.

To be successful, you have to be emotionless. You have to have passion in your business/field, but otherwise, you have to be that asshole who makes the hard choices without remorse. You can't afford to look back and feel bad. If you have to fire that nice guy who has ten kids because he's a total idiot, then you have to do it without hesitation. You hesitate, you lose that moment, and that moment may be the difference between success and failure.

You may feel this is mean, and that as members of an advanced race, we should have a conscience. If we were so advanced, then we wouldn't need money, or material things. We would have transcended these trivial things, and you wouldn't be reading this fay-yoo. But you are, and they are not trivial. In business, any business, you have to be cold, calculating, and not be looking back. When you look back, you trip over the present, and fall into the future. I'd rather be standing up through all of it.

A successful businessperson needs to be like a superior surgeon. They have to cut cancer out, for the good of the body and not give a felgarb about the cancer.

A nice guy is a cancer? Anything that is harming the body, no matter the intention, is bad, and needs to be removed and discarded.

This goes beyond just firing, it also applies to other decisions. The businessperson may have to make the decision to change the company's direction. Many would not be happy with this decision, but the businessperson has to stick with their decision that they think will profit the company the most. This could be going from transporting glitterstim, to ferrying passengers. Or from making sick sticks to making M2019 Blasters.

This also means making the controversial choices. Like mass-producing Gibiril Regimens, even though there may be a 10% failure rate that results in death. Do you make that choice? Can you make that choice? Nine out of ten people will survive and lead a better life, but can you deal with the one that died? Not to the successful businessperson. You would be making profit on all ten people, the one that died, well that's too bad, and you may not get a recommendation from them, but the other nine, they would.

Now you don't go lying (see Honest Businessperson). Tell the truth, but emphasize the benefits, not the drawbacks. You're thinking I'm a sweaty gelignite...I don't care. How many get into the transporter think about the failure rate? Did the manufacturers of the transporter say, "Yeah, great product, gets you where you need to go, but don't try to use it through an electromagnetic field, you may not re-materialize. Oh, and be careful of dense rocks, radiation, microbes, computer failure, ion storms, etc." Uh, no. Emphasizing the positive, downplaying the negative, without letting your conscience get in the way, that is how you become successful, and eventually rich...just don't omit, otherwise you'll be in deep Belgium with lawyers.

Principle 29

Parents have to die. It's the only way children can come into their own.

Don't go out and kill your parents now…that's just messed up. No, here the meaning is more generalized. Parents represent the old ways of doing things, and the people who perpetuate it, and refuse to change. Change is inevitable. It is how we grow, how we learn, how we keep ourselves motivated. If a pool is stagnant, it will at first start teeming with life: bacteria, mosquitoes, Chigs, algae, etc. But after time, it gets choked of life, and the life forms move…Change.

These moves from the old ways don't have to be done on a daily basis; this is done by the unfocused, floundering entities trying to find life. They don't need to have a complete 180 turnaround; these are done by those that need to change their image because they waited too long, or damaged their image. Most companies are neither of these, they are still profitable, have a good market share, and decent image, but in varying degrees. If any of these indicators are inching downwards, a change is needed…we need to stir the pond.

The optimal way of doing this is subtly, small dosages of change over a period of time. If we are too abrupt with our changes, people will resist. It is human nature; we are ugly bags of mostly water that want to find a resting spot to stop the swishing. We like to be comfortable in our routines...but mess with that routine, and we lash out with little regard for logic.

If the "parents" are the employees, they may rebel, but in time, they will realize that they enjoy the pay, and adapt, with grumbling in case the change is bad so that they can say, "See, I knew this was a bad idea!" Hedging their bets. If the "parents" are the ones in charge, the higher ups, change will be harder to adapt, because, as parents, they feel they are always right, so it is better to make them think that this was their idea, or that they had some part in creating this change...egos, stroke them as long as you need them.

If the "parents" are your customers then you need to think of an orderly, innovative plan to implement these changes. It is akin to getting off of dust. You take a little less each day until it is tolerable to get off the stuff and stop frelling with people's minds. You make it imperceptible to your customers. What they don't know, or notice, won't piss them off. Ignorance is bliss, as long as you aren't. You must always be the child constantly killing your parents, and move from the pool to ocean...Ever changing, being the leader. Life depends on change, and renewal.

Principle 30

Outside his own kingdom, the hunter becomes the hunted.

You are not Codru-Ji, so don't try to be one. Most of us have a limited number of limbs, and you can't put your hand in every Jumja jar. Eventually your teeth will rot, and you'll develop diabetes or something. Do what you're good at, what you know. If you start expanding into other markets without knowing what you're doing, well then, you're go-se, and deserve to fail.

Can you succeed in some market that you are ignorant in…yes, but that is called luck, and if you do business in luck, you might as well play the solar lottery. You can take a calculated risk, but in order to do that, you have to have some knowledge in that area. Most merchants will do this, but within the confines of their expertise. The margin of risk therefore is not as great (everyone has different thresholds), but is manageable and will not destroy their business.

You may have multiple proficiencies, but if you spread yourself too thin, you open yourself up to failure due to not being able to give the proper time to each. Pick a few areas, develop, and succeed in those, and once they can be run by others (under your non-micro-managing supervision of course), then you can move to the next areas and be able to devote enough time to those.

If you're not as knowledgeable in what you think is your expertise, or if you say, "Screw it! What does he know! I'm smarter than he is! (Maybe you are, but we'll talk about this ego of yours later)" and go into whatever market is "hot", you will fail. Visitors will come to you and realize that you aren't what you think you are, and eat you alive. Your competitors will see this as well, and use your inexperience in the market to benefit themselves.

Don't chase what is "in", you will always be behind the leader (and you had better hope you aren't too far behind). Let's say a sonic screwdriver has been introduced and is an instant hit, and you decide to get into the market and compete with originator. By the time you develop your own version, about a hundred others will have developed similar devices. You may make money, but it may end up short-lived if one of the other one hundred and one products has a feature or look that yours doesn't, has a better marketing plan, a better distribution network, etc. This doesn't mean you don't go into the market, just have more than a working knowledge of that market (like if you were in on the development of the original or something...although that would make you an engineer, which means you belong below deck).

Another example, without using brand names, is a robot that changes into something of everyday use. There was one company (called "A") that had better knowledge of the consumers, better marketing and branding, and quality. Another company (called "Buhf'es") tried to cash in, called it some other name, did not brand or market as well, had less than superior quality, and made those robots turn into rocks and other stupid things. You may know what happened next..."A" waited until Buhf'es started failing, and at their lowest point, bought them out at a bargain basement price. "A" is still around, Buhf'es is only around as fodder for the "A" robots...and the owners' of Buhf'es...well I don't know, but I haven't heard of them since.

Know your surroundings and you can hunt. If you are in the unknown, move cautiously…and bring a friend who knows.

Principle 31

Listen to the music, not the song.

Ok, this one is kinda deep…I think we should take a break, so relax, reflect upon this, and if you'd like to discuss your thoughts on this quote, email us at either:

jayesh@balanceduniverse.com

or

ranakjones@balanceduniverse.com

Ok, now back to the principles.

Principle 32

Expand, or die.

And I'm not talking about your waistline, or family, or...well, whatever. I'm talking about your business. This goes along with change (see stagnant water). If you go into business thinking that you'll hire seven or eight people, one location, one product, etc, you will fail. You have to go into business thinking that you are starting out with those eight employees, but that soon it will be sixteen, then a million, etc. Why? Because I said so...and if you go into a venture thinking small, you will be small...if you think big, you have a chance to be big. Key word there was chance.

If you only want to make a small amount, or a set amount, then get a job. Just because you think big, don't forget about the small things. Your main objective is to succeed enough to grow. The problem with most small businesses is that their leaders think small, act small, and remain small or non-existent. Even if you are small, it does not mean you have to stay that way. You can use the net to go global or universal. You can always expand into the next spaceport or create complimentary products.

A caveat here is to not grow too big too fast. Come up with plans to expand before you do. Map out how you want to expand, and keep to it. If things go better than expected, you already have a plan to capitalize on it…and if they go worse than expected, you still have a future plan for when things do start to pick up. Let's take the example of Jupster. It took off fast, all the ridgeheads were on it. Then the creator took on some investors just to get more capital. If he had vetted them out better, he would have found that they meddle in the company. Slowly his plans were eroded, and the investors wanted new options put in, even though the old options still needed work. Eventually the ridgeheads moved on because they were frustrated with the direction the company took. Because the inventor tried to infuse money quickly, he lost sight of growing the company at a manageable pace.

Just because you plan for expansion doesn't mean you will. You may want to keep it exclusive, you may be failing for other reasons, or you may be trying to keep a low profile to stay out of a trade guild's attention. If you don't think big, well, then you're small, and if you ever try to expand after the fact, you will do so haphazardly, and probably fail. You will become as extinct as Kataan.

Principle 33

Wanting is more pleasurable than having.

Some may disagree, but if you think about it, you know it is true. This does not mean that having is not pleasurable, just ask someone who's been to Risa, but, the thought of going there creates an anticipation about what you will experience there, and once you get there, it typically will not live up to your preconceived perception of it. If it does, then you will think of the next time, and eventually your wanting will increase beyond the having.

The wanting versus having principle is deeper than just going to a pleasure planet. In business when you have something, you only fight to keep it, but when you want something, you fight for it. You may think there is small to no difference in what I just said. If you do, then fay-yoo. When you fight to keep something, you don't move forward, you are on the defensive. When you fight for something, you go onto the offensive. A person will look more attractive if they are unavailable, if they don't give you the time of day, you want them more, even if you have someone at home…you may not go after them, but they are more alluring. The same with business. You may have a nice little share of thorium sales...but then you see Malastare...and you think how it would be nice to be as big as them.

This should serve as motivation. Use what you have to get what you want, and when you get it, want something more, and so on. This is what drives the powers of the universe, they are never quite satisfied until they have everything, but they secretly don't want it all, because then they will have no more purpose. They need their adversaries to possess some of what they want to keep them moving, keep them wanting. So when you have 10% of the market, want 10% more, and then another 10%, and so on...and when you get to 100%, then move to something else and do it all over again. If you happen to get all of everything, then hand some over to me, and I'll be glad to be your adversary so that you can keep on moving, having a goal.

Principle 34

It's always good business to know about new customers before they walk in the door.

"How do I do that? I don't know who is going to walk in the door?" Neither do I, at least not specifically. You don't need to know everything about them; just enough to make them feel as if you have been expecting them. You know who bought from you yesterday; use that to figure out who would come in today. You build a profile, and each day add to it. If you are selling sweaty gelignite, then you know that your customers will be people who want to blow things up, probably are on the more darker side of politics, and usually will have to pay in cash because you don't want to trust that they won't sneeze and set the felgarb off. You may see other attributes in common, like they wear black or something.

Just knowing who they are is not the whole story here, you have to use what you know about them to create a relationship with them, and ultimately sell to them. The relationship may just be no small talk and get right to the point otherwise they will spend the next half hour telling you their plans, and some goody-goody will come in, vaporize your customer, and you just lost your sale. Of course, with this example we are still talking about a sweaty gelignite dealer. More than likely you are not in this "volatile" business.

Some are not adept at formulating who their customers are (or make the mistake of either over-generalizing or assuming each customer's uniqueness is a generality). For those, there are other companies out there that will put together a profile of your customers…they are called Marketing companies (marketing is not the same as sales, sales is one component of marketing, just as promotions and advertising are components of marketing). If you can't do either, then you're probably a tightwad eema or an idiot.

Knowing your customer saves you and them time, makes the customer feel special, and as long as they like your product, they will come back. It is an old salesperson maneuver to take notes on their customers, so that the next time they try to sell to them, they throw out these tidbits to create the allusion that the customer was more than just a customer, but also someone who is exciting and probably a friend. They may throw out a question about their kids, or how they did in their Pyramid games. Or they may know that the customer likes to get a kick-back or a freebie. The little things are what impress the customers. Knowing these things can mean the difference in making the sale, and quickly, so that you can focus on your next customer.

Principle 35

Understanding is a three-edged sword

Sounds like a T'Pau-ism...but it is a philosophy held on various planets and cultures. I'm sure most have heard about the blind men who came up to an Ingati in the forest, and since none of them had seen one, tried to describe it by feeling it from different sides...if you haven't, then you're probably an engineer, and need to converse more...with real people. If you know the story, go on to the next paragraph...engineers keep reading. One blind man felt its leg, and said this animal is round and furry, and can be held within your arms. The second blind man felt its arms and paws, and described the animal that way, with claws to slice a man. The third blind man felt its ass, and said it was furry, rotund, with a split down the middle, and smells really bad. The fourth blind man, hearing the first three, felt its face...and decided he didn't care about what it looked like, and ran. You must be wondering why the story has four blind men, but we're talking about a three-edged sword...Chichinian math. Seriously, though, it is because the first three made their opinions, and the fourth acted upon it.

Others will tell you to put yourself in your customers shoes, or the customer is always right…boll-yotz! First off, customers always think they are right, but most are entitled idiots (no proof, just an observation). Secondly, yes you put yourself in their shoes, but only one. Keep your shoe on, and then take both off and go to a shoe store and put on a completely different pair, and then you will understand. Ooh, metaphors. You need to know your perspective, the other's perspective, and then need to step back, and look at the situation as if you don't have a personal stake in it. Easily said, but hard to do.

Not all of us are erudite like that. So how do we, the lay-class, use this principle? What you need to do is not think of this as black and white, but various shades of gray. And then take as many of those shades to get as close to the perfect shade of gray. For example, a customer comes to you and says that your product is the most expensive they've seen. You find and contact your competitors and find out what they are selling the product for. You compare it to yours. You may find your price is higher than most, therefore the customer's perception was correct. You may find your price is relatively the same as everybody else's, then you need to find out why this customer thinks that way, like maybe they're trying to get you to lower your price to get a deal. You may also find that you have the lowest price, therefore coming to the conclusion that the customer must be, at least partly Neimoidian.

This principle builds upon the knowledge principle referred to earlier, the more points of view you have, the better you will be able to understand, and once you understand, you can bend it to your advantage. For example, if you already knew your competitor's prices and you let the customer know of all the ones that are more expensive than you, or if you have knowledge of their quality, or lack of, you can let them know that you get what you pay for.

Principle 36

The justification for profit is profit.

No, this is not a gecko-ism. We aren't talking about greed. This is purely about profit. You do not need to justify that your company is making money. There are no excuses. It is there to benefit you…yeah, I know, since when is profit not there to benefit the profiteers? Never. You do not need to apologize, or feel guilty. Again, this sounds like a no-brainer, but you will be surprised to find out that there are those out there that want you to have a reason to be making money. Or if you have a lot already, then they want you to donate here or there. Why? Because it'll make you look like a good person? How long will that last, a day, a year?

The more you make, the more people feel you shouldn't, or you should share it. They want you to give handouts…but how many handouts did you get? This is not about them, but you. If you want to give money to some "worthy" cause, it should be up to you, not because of how much you made. You may have different reasons for giving, such as tax write-offs, you actually want to help out, to make you seem benevolent, for status, or to grease some palms. Whatever the reason, they should come from what you want to do, not because someone thinks that you need to justify your profits.

The reason this principle is here is to let you know that greed may be there, but that is also not a justification for the profit. Profit is to help you make more profit. You can use it to re-invest into your company. Or use it to come up with new products. Or to pay dividends to your investors to make your company look more attractive to future investors. Or to buy yourself a politician or two to pass favorable laws. Or to hire the Thenta Makur to off your competitors. Whatever the reason, profit should be used to make more profit...and if you have some extra left over, then good for you.

"Well, what about me? I want to use the profits to buy myself stuff, and live the good life!" Well, that will also help to make more profits. When you have materialistic ways, you will push yourself to maintain your spending habits, or keep up your lavish lifestyle. Plus, if you're hobnobbing with the Eloi, that will help you network yourself, and possibly create other streams of profit. The point is, profit needs no excuses, needs no justification. It is an entity that needs no forgiveness.

Principle 37

The one who believes that they are more important than others only demonstrates that their opinion is to be ignored.

The very powerful and the very stupid have one thing in common. They don't alter their views to fit the facts. They alter the facts to fit their views. Even those entities with a positronic brain are wrong sometimes, so why believe that you have the most important opinion? We've all heard the blowhards spouting their opinions, and when someone tries to posit a differing opinion, they are shot down, usually with said blowhard not letting the others defend their position, or confounding the issue with unrelated information. Whether they are right or wrong, they should be ignored and not be given the position of power.

This goes for the businessperson as well. It only makes sense to actively seek out other's opinions, and not to hold themselves above others. This goes along with the "three-edged sword" and the "knowledge" principles. The more info you have, the better decision you can make. When you let ego guide you, you will fail. Ego should not be confused with confidence, which you need. Egos will discount a valid point or opinion because it does not conform to its opinion. For example, there was this politician who had all sorts of power, and he felt he could convince any perceived threat to join him, and that no one would ever betray him. When the son of one of his most trusted men started to ascend, he felt that he could convince this young man to join him. He offered him everything, power, position, etc. He even enlisted his father to convince him. The son said that his father would betray him, and the politician just laughed, called him foolish, and threatened to destroy the son. Well, the father betrayed the politician (obviously, if he didn't, this example would be pointless). The politician was destroyed, and the son and his sister ended up with all the power. If only the politician had listened.

If you are reading this book, you probably are not very powerful. Therefore, do not alter the facts to fit your opinions, and don't think that you are so important that your dren doesn't stink. Listen to, and ask for, other's opinions, and hold them up as important as yours…if everything is important, then it is all unimportant.

If you are reading this book, then you are not very stupid. If you learn from this, then you probably aren't stupid either. My opinion is learn…but I'm open to your opinions…unless you are a greebol.

Principle 38

Never confuse wisdom with luck.

Why is that? They're millionaires, billionaires even; they must be doing something right. Right? No. Just because a person makes millions on an idea, does not make them wise. Let's exclude the brats that inherited their fortunes and try to make a living off of the names of their mommies and daddies. Let's also exclude winners of lotteries or other light gambling. Now we have these millionaires, let's see how they got there…nah, don't want to waste our time going over all of their histories. We'll just take some examples and go from there…of course we will not be using real names of people, aliens, companies, or products…they have a lot of money, and can sue my ass off, or at least keep me in courts for a long time. And that's not drad.

Let's first talk about the Millionaire who went to the Officer's Academy and hobnobbed with the rich and famous there, and somehow came up with an idea (actually "borrowed" it from someone else), and made millions. Was he wise? Only in that he was smart enough to claim the idea as his, and because of the stupidity of the others, ponied up with investors that used their money to squelch the "competitor". He was smart enough to take the idea to someone who could help him market it. He was smart enough to keep his mouth shut until the last minute so no copyright laws could be used (got his product out before the others could, and since they had nothing in writing prior, they lose). He was wise, but also very lucky. The idea he "borrowed" was actually out there before, he just came up with a catchy name, and a few redesigns. It took off, but it could have easily fallen by the wayside if his timing was off just a siuren. Did I also mention that he had money, just not millionaire money, but was well off, and could hobnob with the rich? Luck, that he was born with a 50% silver spoon in his mouth. Luck that he was at the Officer's Academy and had common friends with the competitors. Luck that the idea fell into his lap. He was wise in a devious, unethical way, which is not wrong, and not always without its consequences, but the rest…luck.

Another example is this veruul who went into his father's housing business. He moved to the business district in a large city, and saw an opportunity to build larger, attractive qach. He was right, and made a lot of money. Wise. But then later on, started building gambling dens, financed by junk bonds and other loans. And kept taking out loans, until he was so far in debt, he had to file for bankruptcy. Not wise. But luckily he was able to remain on the board, in name only, but lost controlling interest. Where is the luck in this? After all of that, he still acted rich, hobnobbed with them, and because of this, his name was still synonymous with wealth. He was able to caché that into a show, and re-establish his wealth based on his supposed wisdom in business. How wise are you if you've had to declare bankruptcy…twice. He was lucky that the masses believe his Ilhrei'sian shtick.

The point is, just because someone is rich and/or successful, does not make them wise. Or make everything that they say or do wise, even if they have done some wise things before. What makes one wise is experience, and learning from those experiences, good and bad. Some of the wisest people live in remote swamp planets…or the ten brothers whose names all sound the same.

Principle 39

You are one among many.

Your parents, teachers, TV shows, counselors, girlfriend/boyfriend/alienfriend, and The Book of Pythia lied to you. You are not special. You are one of many. You are replaceable. You say, "Well my mommy told me I am one of a kind! And she never lies!" or "My spouse is one of a kind, there is no replacing them!" or maybe "Frack you! Nobody is like me!" Well go back to suckling on...well, you know. And by the way, how lame are you for using "frack"! I'm not talking strictly personal, but mainly business. Some will say they are unique, and no one sells their product. I say those people are engineers. Damned engineers think because they add a nullifier core to the propulsion system, then they are unique.

Let's take that propulsion system, and let's say our engineer friends actually do something useful and increase its efficiency to 99.999% by adding said nullifier core. Does this make it unique? Yes. Does it make it irreplaceable? No. You may not find another propulsion system that is as efficient, but you will be able to find another propulsion system. And if only the one company makes a nuclear propulsion system, you can always get an anti-gravity propulsion system to move your vessel. It may not be what you want, but it will get you to where you need. There is always a replacement.

"Well I have an iTricorder, and that's irreplaceable!" Well whoop-de-doo! You take away the name, and look at the insides, it has similar tech to the regular tricorders. Just because the iTri comes in a cooler package does not make it irreplaceable. It makes it a luxury. It makes it a fad. It can be replaced. There are literally hundreds of different tricorders out there. They may not have the same options, or, guay, have any options, but they all can scan, and that's the main point.

This doesn't mean you don't have a marketing angle to selling your merchandise. The iTri's market themselves as being unique, that are for the unique, creative, and cool. The fact that almost half of all tricorders sold are iTri's, and really not all that unique is moot. They've positioned themselves in that way. They keep their pricing simple, and a little high. They always make less than what is demanded, to make the consumer feel like there is a limited amount of the iTri's. Perception has more influence than reality.

The point is that you need to remember that your product/company is one of many, and that some customers know this. You need to make them, and any others who may start to realize this, to think that you are not, that you are unique. You need to make your employees think that you are unique. Perception is what can make your business unique. Once they have all assimilated to the fact of uniqueness, you must remember you are not.

Principle 40

Always have sex with the boss. Never have sex with the boss's sister.

Not literally…well maybe, if they're some hot greenskin or something. Here the sex part is the most important. The "bosses" are your consumers, your vendors, etc. Basically anyone you interact with. You could try to literally sleep with all of them…but I think you wouldn't really get much done. No, you need to sell sex. Everyone, even engineers, know that sex sells, but they also think it is limited to advertising. While this is a nice medium to proliferate sex, it is not the only place.

Have you ever noticed on diplomatic missions, inevitably you will have at least one very attractive female especially when meeting with an all male contingent? Or vice versa? Of course it is to curry favorable results. So how do you use this in a business meeting (see empty stomach mentioned earlier)? Bring a good looking female or male, depending on your audience. No actual zarking need be required, but just the tease of it will render your audience dumbstruck.

Sometimes the sexual can be in overtones. Obviously, in advertising this is much more straightforward. You can use suggestive language to entice your audience. You can also use sexually attractive vocals. Or maybe you can model your phaser after a "male organ" for females and androgynes ...why am I making this G? Drannit, drannit, drannit. There I feel better. Or you could make different sized phasers, and sell the largest to the males who fly around in the Yacht-class starships. Or to the females who look lonely. Okay, we're getting a bit off base here. Let's move on.

So we've talked about physical sex, oral sex (for the unenlightened that's verbal), sexual designs, visual overtones...what's left? Well what if you have a product that is unsexy, cannot be designed to look like body parts, or can't afford a Sihnon? How can you use sex in your business? There are other things you can do to make things "sexy", like using appetizing colors.

Colors can influence people more than they think. Red is associated with feelings of love, warmth, and comfort. It can also be associated with excitement and intensity. Blue creates feelings of calmness or serenity. It can also elicit sadness or aloofness. It is also considered the least appetizing color, even though it is considered the favorite color by most people, especially men. Green is often thought of as a symbol of fertility, and is relaxing. Orange is considered an energetic color, and elicits feelings of excitement, enthusiasm, and warmth. This list can go on, but I think you get the idea. Colors can set the tone for your product, or its advertising.

There are other things you can use to make your product sexy, such as sounds, touch, smell, etc. You can also use these to make sales, whether it is some greenskin, making the scenery around where the sale is being made more appealing (greenskins are good for that as well), having pleasant smells around your prospects, etc. The feelings of sex will relax your prospects, and make them make decisions without proper blood flow to the brain.

Principle 41

Fate's a bitch.

And here we are, the last principle of this book, the climax, the end all, be all. Fate is a bitch. Even with all the planning and use of principles, this one can really zark things up. And we aren't talking about preordained destiny, or some divine being or beings already deciding how things will end up. Guay, what being would care to "write" down all of our destinies, and then let them play out? That'd be like writing a mystery novel, and then reading it to make sure none of the characters step out of place. If everything is preordained, then why try to do anything, it's already going to happen whether you do nothing or everything, so why fight. The stumps, dirt eaters, monads, and bulletheads would all agree, things are not foretold; we need to actively create our own destinies. Let's get out of the religious ramifications here, and talk about this in terms of business.

First, things will happen that you have no control over. War could break out tomorrow between the Goblyns and Drakhs. A common virus could mutate today to destroy the whole Ancients civilization. An earthquake devastates your suppliers. So on and so forth. Second, your consumers may decide your product is no longer cool, or is obsolete, or is da-shiong bao-jah-shr duh la doo-tze. Customers are fickle, what they want today, tomorrow they want to ban. Third, your timing could be off, and some other son of a tralk comes out with a better product the day before you come out with yours.

With all that could go wrong unexpectedly, how can you protect yourself? Well, don't get caught unawares. Have a plan for as many "unexpected" occurrences that fate throws at you. Even if you do, you can't predict when it will happen, and you can't predict everything. Sometimes you have to take the hit, accept it, and move on. The more you dwell on something that's happened, that you can't go back in time and change (unless you're a Timelord), the more you waste your time. Don't put all your eggs in one basket And, yes, I remember telling you about the hunter being the hunted, doesn't mean you can't get into another domain that you do know about, or entrust someone else who may have experience in the other domain. Also, keep some of your credits aside, so even if you lose your business, you still have enough to start in some other business. You could also set up your business as some liability-free organization; the exactness would depend on what planet you're from.

In the end, fate may be a bitch, but it doesn't mean you have to let it make you its bitch.

About the Authors:

Jayesh Mehta is marketing professional. He has either owned or worked as a consultant for four different successful ventures. His passion for writing started when he was thirteen. He had refused to print his materials until recently. He has written over 500 poems/songs, 1 play, 3 fiction stories, and with this book, 1 non-fiction book. His topics are varied, with differing styles.

For more information please visit: www.balanceduniverse.com

Ranak Jones is a wanderer. He occasionally lectures at various street corners and parks. He is blunt and opinionated. He hates ants.

For more information please visit, nowhere.

NOTES:

PITOH:

筆記:

Bǐjì:

blm:

.

www.ingramcontent.com/pod-product-compliance
Lightning Source LLC
Chambersburg PA
CBHW022130170626
46808CB00002B/935